Original title:
The Oak That Told Stories

Author: Matthew Whitaker
ISBN HARDBACK: 978-1-80567-288-3
ISBN PAPERBACK: 978-1-80567-587-7

Wisdom Etched in Bark

In the woods where stories blend,
A wise old tree makes friends.
With knots and grooves, it shares a laugh,
Of squirrels and birds that take a bath.

One branch swings low with a mighty joke,
Of how he once was a fence post oak.
His rings reveal the secrets he keeps,
While chatting with deer during their sleeps.

Nature's Archive of Chronicles

In a forest thick with tales,
The trees chuckle, turn their gales.
Squirrels gossip, birds will chime,
Every season, a new rhyme.

Frogs leap in, sharing a jest,
While the sun laughs, giving its best.
Grass blades sway, whisper and tease,
Nature's humor floats on the breeze.

Leaves That Speak in Shadows

When shadows dance on stone-cold ground,
The leaves engage in chatter profound.
They gossip about the clouds up high,
And trade old secrets that make them sigh.

With fluttering jokes in whispers of green,
They ponder the oddest things they've seen.
A chipmunk's curious like a sleuth at night,
As tales spin 'round with delight and fright.

Arbor’s Embrace of Time

In the shade of the ancient, tall and grand,
Time plays tricks, oh so unplanned.
The grass grows green with tales of the past,
As rabbits hop by, racing fast.

With every leaf that rustles and sways,
There's mischief stirred in amusing ways.
The stories unfold as branches sway free,
In a world where laughter grows like a tree.

The Timbered Talekeeper

Beneath a bough, the tales unwind,
Of pirate ships and ducks that whined.
A woodpecker knocks to join the fun,
While critters gather, one by one.

With a twisty trunk that loves to boast,
He spins wild yarns of a ghostly toast.
Each creak and crack is a giggle shared,
In this wooden haven, nobody's scared.

The Sage Under the Canopy

Beneath the leaves, a wise old tree,
Tells of antics and jubilee.
With every rustle, a giggle lends,
Giving life to the forest's trends.

Raccoons dance, the owls will wink,
Bouncing tales that make you think.
Creatures gather for laughs to share,
In this nurturing, leafy lair.

Voices of the Verdant Keep

Whispers rise from roots so deep,
Among the branches, secrets peep.
Bunnies snicker, while snakes debate,
Who’s the fastest in this slate.

Butterflies flit, with colors bright,
Sharing jokes from morning to night.
The wind joins in with playful sighs,
As laughter echoes through the skies.

Remnants of Stories Past

A log lies down with cracks to show,
Tales of laughter from long ago.
Mice replay every little prank,
While beetles hold a comedy rank.

The shadows stretch and twist to play,
Reflecting stories in their way.
The lighthearted past comes alive,
In this memory, we all thrive.

Leaves of Lament and Joy

Once there was a leaf that wept,
It had too many jokes, no one kept.
Its giggles echoed through the breeze,
Making squirrels lose their nuts with ease.

But joy turned yellow, fell on the ground,
Those puns of laughter, all around.
The wind just blew, without a care,
While cardinals chuckled, perched up there.

Echoing Through the Ages

An acorn spoke of days so bright,
With whispers of laughter in the night.
It told of critters, wise and bold,
Who danced under stars, stories told.

But trees can be quite the gossipers,
The branches shake with silly whispers.
Echoes of laughter spin and twirl,
In a comedy caper, chaos will swirl.

The Tall Tales of Timber

A log once claimed it saw the moon,
Said it danced to a crazy tune.
The bark was thick, but tales were taller,
With each twist, the forest would holler.

Woodpeckers joined in with a beat,
Making mischief, oh what a feat!
That timber knew how to spin a yarn,
Leaving the stars both shocked and charmed.

Tales Written in the Fabric of Nature

Amongst the roots where secrets brew,
A wise old twig whispered something new.
Stories of breezes, giggling and sly,
While dandelions laughed as clouds went by.

With twigs and vines, they made a scene,
The forests chuckled, oh what a routine!
Nature's laughter stitched throughout the land,
In patterns of humor, ever so grand.

Whispers between Leaves and Sky

In the branches, secrets swing,
Squirrels mock with tiny bling.
A bird's gossip rings afar,
While ants dance under a leaf star.

The wind giggles through the boughs,
Ticklish tales from nature's cows.
A leaf falls with a playful twist,
"I've seen things that you have missed!"

Timeless Tales from the Green World

Mossy legends, wise and bold,
About a worm who dared be old.
With a grin, it claimed the moat,
Said, "I'm the king of all remote!"

The sun chuckled, painted gold,
While shadows danced, stories told.
A beetle boasts of distant lands,
While grasshoppers form bands of bands.

Legends that Dance with the Wind

Dandelions spread tales so spry,
Winking at clouds as they float by.
A chattering squirrel takes the lead,
With nuts of wisdom, it plants a seed.

A gust of breeze, a feather's flight,
Whispers of mischief, pure delight.
The blades of grass nod with glee,
As stories swirl in jubilee.

The Oral History of the Forest's Heart

In the heart where shadows play,
A raccoon tells tales in a cheeky way.
With paws up high, it claims its fame,
"I found the finest fig—what a game!"

The owls hoot, wise and bright,
While crickets share their zestful flight.
A root whispers to a sprout,
"Let's write a story, without a doubt!"

Hidden Histories Underneath

Roots weave tangled tales below,
Of squirrels plotting their next show.
There’s gossip in the silent ground,
Where secrets of the forest abound.

A hedgehog claims he found a shoe,
Belonging to a giant, too!
Wise old ants form a council grand,
Deciding if they’ll take a stand.

An owl hoots humor, full of sass,
While badgers in the bushes pass.
If only trees could raise a brow,
They’d laugh at tales from here and now.

A Canopy of Whispers

Above, the leaves like chatter dance,
While birds take turns at their romance.
A parrot jokes; it's quite a show,
Squirrels giggle, 'Watch him go!'

In shadows deep, a family of gnomes,
Crafting hats from ancient foams.
Their meetings held at dusk's soft peek,
With mushroom chairs and cozy sneak.

Branches bend to hear the tease,
As breezes carry on with ease.
The laughter rolls like rippling streams,
In this world spun from whimsical dreams.

Tales Woven Through the Seasons

Spring brings chatter about new blooms,
With ladybugs making quaint rooms.
While summer's sun ignites a spree,
Where ants throw picnics on a tree.

Autumn leaves with colors bright,
Share tales of berry-biting nights.
The wind tells jokes, a playful beast,
As harvest creeps up like a feast.

Winter wraps in frosty layers,
With snowflakes weaving songs of prayers.
A moose tells tales of battles won,
While twinkling stars glow just for fun.

Lore of the Whispering Leaves

Whispers echo through the night,
Of critters' shenanigans in flight.
A raccoon sporting a silly hat,
Sneaks by the owl, oh imagine that!

That spider spins webs with great flair,
Crafting stories beyond compare.
With every thread a secret spun,
In this wild world, there's endless fun!

Leaves laugh softly in the breeze,
At tales of wizards lost with keys.
If only ears could pause and hear,
The juicy gossip far and near.

Fables Beneath Starlit Canopies

In the night, the tales arise,
Squirrels gossip 'neath moonlit skies.
A raccoon shares a laugh or two,
While fireflies dance in a swirling queue.

The owl hoots softly, wise and slow,
While crickets chirp a funny show.
The trees lean in, with branches wide,
As laughter echoes, side by side.

A hedgehog winks, with spiky grace,
With each new story, smiles they trace.
While shadows flicker, hearts grow bold,
In fables woven, laughter's gold.

As dawn approaches, tales take flight,
In every bark, a giggle, bright.
The woods alive, with humor sweet,
Under the stars, where friends all meet.

Echos from the Enchanted Boughs

Beneath the limbs, the secrets sway,
Whispers of mischief, night and day.
A rabbit hops with a cheeky grin,
While a clever fox slips quietly in.

With each creak and crack of the wood,
The stories tumble, all in good mood.
A parrot squawks a punchline clear,
While laughter rises, far and near.

The leaves shake gently, as if to tease,
Tickling tales danced by a breeze.
With every rustle, humor flows,
From the branches, joy only grows.

So gather 'round, oh curious hearts,
In this realm where whimsy starts.
Among the roots and knotted stones,
Echoes of laughter, our happy tones.

Interlacing Lives in Solitude

Under the branches, stories spin,
A badger prances with a toothy grin.
With tales of blunders and playful jests,
The forest listens, and truly invests.

The breeze chuckles as squirrels chase,
Each leap and twist, a comic grace.
A lizard blinks, with a sly remark,
As shadows dance in the growing dark.

The patchwork lives blend and tease,
In this solitude, all find ease.
From acorns, laughter too can grow,
In every corner, jokes on show.

So join the feast, oh merry friends,
In these woods where mirth transcends.
Intertwined hearts, through thick and thin,
In every giggle, life’s a win.

The Storyweaver Among the Woods

In the glade, where shadows twine,
A storyteller spins her vine.
With every word, a creature sways,
Lost in laughter 'til the end of days.

A chipmunk chuckles, as tales unfold,
Of daring deeds and mischief bold.
While wanderers pause 'neath the leafy dome,
Each fable sung feels like home.

The toad croaks rhythms, a little off-key,
But together, they create a symphony.
With tales of blunders, dear and true,
In every chuckle, the magic grew.

So gather near, and lend an ear,
For whimsy thrives 'round laughter here.
Spinning yarns, both bright and odd,
As nature weaves her charm, so broad.

Ancestral Echoes in the Glade

Once there stood a tree, oh so wise,
Whispering tales 'neath the sunlit skies.
Squirrels took notes on a twiggy pad,
While birds would chirp, 'Ain't that a fad?'

Its roots held secrets from ages past,
Of dancing critters who moved so fast.
The shadows laughed with a rustling sound,
As laughter and stories swirled all around.

The Storytelling Grove

In a grove where giggles are all the rage,
Stories unfold on each living page.
A rabbit wore glasses, quite proud of that,
While a turtle dreamed big in a tiny hat.

They'd gather at dusk for a tale or two,
As the fireflies glimmered like stars that flew.
A raccoon recited a far-fetched lore,
That left all the friends rolling on the floor.

Timeless Chronicles of the Woods

Beneath the boughs, the gossip ran wild,
As the old sage owl shared stories unfiled.
A squirrel claimed he once won a race,
With a snail, no less, in a most nimble chase!

The woods would shake with each gleeful jest,
As rabbits and foxes laughed at their best.
They'd nod to the tree, the wise ol' sage,
Who chuckled and winked, turning another page.

Folklore from the Forest Floor

On the forest floor, where the fun never stops,
Frogs told tales that made the owl hop.
A bear played the drum with a big furry paw,
Twisting the truth with a playful guffaw.

They spoke of mishaps, of comical blunders,
How raccoons raided and caused wild wonders.
Leaves fluttered down like confetti bright,
As laughter echoed deep into the night.

Whispers of the Evergreen

In a forest bright and green,
Lived a tree, quite the scene.
With a grin and a twist,
Stories swirled in the mist.

Squirrels gathered, tails in a knot,
Listening close, enjoying the plot.
Birds chirped jokes, oh what a sight,
Laughter echoed, day and night.

Tales Unfurled in the Forest's Embrace

Beneath a crown of leafy glee,
A chap with bark told tales, you see.
With rustling leaves, he'd laugh and cheer,
Spinning stories, far and near.

A rabbit bounced, with ears so tall,
Said, "Tell me of the great big fall!"
The tree replied with a playful swing,
"Oh, you should see what squirrels bring!"

Reflections Under the Ancient Shade

In shadows long, where critters played,
An old tree sat, with sunlight displayed.
He shared his tales of yesteryear,
With chuckles deep and hearty cheer.

A fox in glasses, quite the sight,
Said, "That story gave me quite a fright!"
The tree just laughed, with a rumbling tone,
"Wait 'til you hear how I lost my cone!"

Murmurs from the Woodland Spirit

Amongst the ferns, in a gentle breeze,
A spirit whispered, as light as cheese.
"Gather round, it's tale time, friends!"
As giggles spread, the joy transcends.

The owl hooted, wise and smooth,
"What tales today have you to soothe?"
The spirit chuckled, swirling about,
"Just wait for the punchline — it'll knock you out!"

Legends from the Heartwood

In the glade where whispers play,
Old roots dance in a silly sway.
Branches twist with tales absurd,
While acorns chuckle, oh so heard.

Squirrels gossip and share their fame,
Each nut’s a joke, each tree a game.
Leaves chuckle softly in the breeze,
Nature's laughter, sure to please.

Woodpeckers tap with witty remarks,
Jokes about the sun and sparks.
Beneath the boughs, a fairytape,
Wonders woven, dreams take shape.

When dusk descends, the shadows dance,
A nightly show, a silly chance.
The heartwood sings with a playful tune,
Underneath the smiling moon.

Remnants of the Forest's Memory

In the thicket where stories blend,
Worn logs giggle, their backs they bend.
Roots recount adventures bold,
Of critters lost, and treasure told.

Mushrooms chuckle with glee and mirth,
As they share of their fungal birth.
A chipmunk's tale of a daring race,
Leaves the others rolling, joy on their face.

Raccoons plan pranks under moon's glow,
A scheme to steal, a shiny bow.
Echoes of laughter, from branch to brook,
Whimsical stories in every nook.

Time stands still, a silly scene,
As shadows dance, oh so keen.
The whispers of the forest sing,
As nature's chorus takes to wing.

Fables of the Sturdy Sentinel

In a grove where the tall tales tower,
Trunks canoodle with leaves in power.
Bark has jokes that truly appeal,
While creatures plot their next big steal.

A badger boasts of a clever ruse,
Involving honey, a bear, and snooze.
With every story, a giggle's grown,
As saplings snicker, their laughter honed.

Ants parade in a comical drill,
Carrying crumbs up the golden hill.
The mighty sentinel, wise and grand,
Grins down on the humor of the land.

At twilight, the tales spin and glide,
With breezy whispers, laughter rides.
Each rustic charm holds a quirky glee,
In every ring, a history.

Voices Carried on the Breeze

When the wind blows through the leafy rows,
Funny voices echo, as the fun grows.
Swaying branches with secrets untold,
Tickle the heart with adventures bold.

A crow caws jokes from the treetop high,
While weary travelers stop by to sigh.
Even the stones join in the fun,
With whispers swirling, in rays of sun.

A merry band of critters convene,
Sharing stories, silly and serene.
Each flick of a tail and cheeky glance,
Sets the stage for a raucous dance.

As twilight winks and stars appear,
The forest sings with joy, oh dear!
With laughter echoing on every breeze,
Nature’s jesters put minds at ease.

The Archive of Silent Roots

In a grove where giggles grow,
Roots of wisdom twist below.
Squirrels chat with tales of yore,
Branching out from mythic lore.

Whispers tickle, softly sung,
Nature's gags have just begun.
Bees buzz jokes as they hum by,
While sleepy snails just roll their eyes.

Mushrooms laugh, with caps so round,
As vines weave stories, tight and bound.
Old logs chuckle, cracked and wise,
Sharing secrets 'neath the skies.

With every rustle, a punchline waits,
Pulling giggles from the fates.
In this quirky, leafy place,
The roots hold wisdom with a grin on face.

Fables of a Whispering Grove

In the grove where whispers gleam,
Saplings plot and giggle, scheme.
A rabbit tells of tricks and pranks,
While turtles nod and roll their flanks.

Branches sway, with humor keen,
Jokes unfold where few have been.
Acorns drop, and laughter's spread,
As shadows dance on stories said.

The owl hoots a riddle loud,
While butterflies flit, feeling proud.
Every leaf's a page turned bright,
In sunlit air, joy takes flight.

From crackling twigs, they shout and play,
As critters join the fun ballet.
In this realm of giggling cheer,
Fables sprout, year after year.

Memories Trapped in Twigs

Twigs recall the tales of yesteryear,
Of dancing squirrels and skies so clear.
With every crack, a story told,
Of acorns lost and legends bold.

Bushy tails flick, mischief afoot,
While the fox claims, “I’m the best tooot!”
Leaves join in with a rustling jest,
In this playful grove, they know no rest.

A playful breeze carries the sound,
Of laughter echoing all around.
Dragonflies join the playful chase,
As funny memories fill the space.

Whenever sunbeams paint the ground,
Laughter echoes, sweet and profound.
In twigs and leaves, the fun's alive,
Where giggles blossom and stories thrive.

Chronicles of the Leafy Sentinel

In branches thick, a guardian grins,
With leaves that dance as mischief spins.
Each rustle echoes a cheeky tale,
Of startled deer and cheeky quail.

The sentinel gazes, wise and sly,
As mushrooms giggle and fireflies fly.
Crickets chirp a nightly song,
In humor's realm, they all belong.

Every shadow, a tale unfolds,
Of hidden treasures and antics bold.
With moonlight shining through the boughs,
The stories linger, laughter bows.

Tickling winds shake each leaf's heart,
As creatures play their funny part.
In this leafy realm, oh what fun,
The chronicles shine bright as the sun.

Chronicles of the Timbered Sage

In the woods where laughter grows,
A sage with roots and leafy prose.
He chuckles at the passing deer,
And shares his tales of yesteryear.

With squirrels gathered, gaming sounds,
He spins the wildest stories 'round.
A talking trunk with bark so wise,
He winks and tells of clouded skies.

The frogs all croak in giggly fits,
As he recalls his youthful fits.
With acorns falling like confetti,
His punchlines hit—oh, they are petty!

So if you stroll beneath his shade,
Listen close, don't be afraid.
For in each knot and twist of grain,
Are tales of joy, love, and some pain.

Echoes of the Woodland Elder

Beneath the sun, where shadows play,
An elder's jokes brighten the day.
With every gust, his laughter rings,
A symphony of bird-like flings.

He tells of rivers full of cheese,
Of dancing clouds and chocolate trees.
The critters gather, tails a-twitch,
As they await his next wild pitch.

With branches low, he leans in near,
Shadows casting, never fear.
Tales of giants who couldn't dance,
And a snail who had a love's romance.

So journey forth to meet his stare,
A woodland sage with stories rare.
In each bark crevice, laughter's glow,
As legends spin where breezes blow.

Secrets Spun in Leaves

Amidst the rustle, giggles rise,
A whispering tree with crafty ties.
It chuckles secrets, old and new,
Of magical frogs in a bright blue hue.

With every flutter, stories bloom,
Of frisky foxes in a room.
They dance on roots beneath the ground,
In this shrine of fun, laughter is found.

Raccoons listen, wide-eyed, surprised,
To tales of mischief, bold and disguised.
Each leaf flutters with pure delight,
As the sun sets, giving night its light.

So pluck a leaf, let giggles show,
In this realm, where secrets flow.
For every whisper from the tree,
Is a giggle shared in harmony.

Narratives of the Gnarled Branches

Gnarled and twisted, with arms outspread,
This tree has tales that dance in your head.
He shrugs at storms that pass him by,
And tosses jokes up to the sky.

A squirrel, perched, can't keep his glee,
When tales of spoons as boats are free.
Of ants who dreamed of being kings,
And birds that raced on tiny wings.

His branches sway, a rabble-rouser,
Sharing tales that make you louder.
With tickling winds, he spins his yarns,
Of lovebirds wooing 'neath the stars.

So pause a while, enjoy the shade,
Let laughter linger, never fade.
In each gnarled twist, a jest awaits,
In the laughter of the woodland's gates.

The Gnarled Storyteller

With branches wide and arms outstretched,
He chirps a tale, a little fetched.
A squirrel once lost its acorn stash,
Tripped on a root and made quite a crash!

He chuckles low, his leaves a-twitch,
Of bunnies who danced, not a single hitch.
Their hops caught raindrops, like pearls on a string,
Who knew such antics the forest could bring?

A raccoon recounts, with a wink and a grin,
How he stole some fruit from a neighborly kin.
But the owl was watching, a wise old chap,
"Better run fast! You'll end up in a trap!"

So gather round, let the stories unwind,
Of critters and tales that are silly and kind.
This gnarled old tree has laughter to lend,
With every little whisper, the fun never ends.

Shadows of Yesteryears

In shadows that slip, a tale takes flight,
Of a hedgehog who danced on a warm summer night.
He pranced on the grass, feeling so bold,
Until a quick tumble had him turning cold!

With each little giggle, the fireflies danced,
While frogs croaked a tune, as if they had pranced.
"The best things," said a turtle, "are often quite odd,
Like the way you just flopped, you silly little clod!"

The moon chuckled too, its glow full and bright,
As stories rolled out in the cool silver light.
Of critters who argued, over a piece of cheese,
"Just share it, you fools! It'll bring us such ease!"

So linger awhile, let laughter take hold,
For these shadows of yesteryears never grow old.
They twist and they turn like branches in jest,
Spinning old tales that we love the best.

Silhouettes of Forgotten Echoes

In the twilight glow, shadows start to glow,
A rabbit recalls his misstep in tow.
He hopped with such glee, on a log slick and damp,
Then faceplanted hard, like a great comic stamp!

A fox burst in laughter, with a clever little quip,
"Better watch where you hop, or you'll end up in a dip!"
The stories unfold like leaves on a breeze,
Whiskers twitching, everyone giggles with ease.

Then came a wise hen, with feathers so proud,
"Of all my adventures, have I told you aloud?
Of chasing my tail in a scamper so spry,
Resulting in fluffs when I aimed for the sky?"

These silhouettes dance, as echoes replay,
Tales wrap around like a blanket they sway.
With each twist and turn, the laughter will spark,
Stories in shadows, in the light of the dark.

Wisdom Carried by the Breeze

The breeze brings a chuckle from tall sage above,
Whispers of antics that sprawl like a glove.
Of a wise old crow who cawed with a grin,
Stealing hats from strangers, oh where to begin!

A raccoon in shades gives a sly little wink,
"I swear on my paws, I don't even blink!"
Then a turtle chimed in, with laughs hard to hold,
"Maybe it's time to be less brave and bold!"

Each gust carries stories, antics so bright,
Of frogs in tuxedos, a sight full of light.
Dancing through reeds, oh how they can boogie,
Who knew a frog could be so very groovy?

So listen a while, let the breeze be your guide,
To laughter-filled tales that are swirling inside.
Wisdom and giggles float free in the air,
Spreading joy like sunshine, everywhere!

Glistening Gifts of Time's Passage

In the shade, the squirrels dance,
With acorns tucked in their pants.
Each nut a secret from the past,
They giggle, thinking they're so fast.

A rabbit hops, so smart and spry,
Telling tales of clouds up high.
The leaves all rustle in delight,
As critters gather for their night.

The wise old tree just shakes its head,
While crickets play a tune instead.
With branches swaying, it's a show,
Of laughter, whispers, and a glow.

And when the moon begins to rise,
The shadows dance before our eyes.
In this glen, with light so fine,
Even time enjoys a glass of wine.

Ancestral Voices in the Oaks

Beneath the limbs of wisdom tall,
Old leaves recount the funny fall.
A squirrel misspelled its name in bark,
Echoes from when the world was dark.

Birds gather round, with chirps and tweets,
Sharing tales of funny feats.
A fox once tripped, and what a sight,
Flew right into a bush at night.

The branches shake with laughter loud,
As woodland creatures gather 'round.
“Remember when?” becomes the phrase,
In the oaky hug of sunny days.

So here we sit with drinks in hand,
Among the laughter, ever grand.
The tree just smiles, its bark so wise,
In ancient tales, it finds surprise.

Stories Passed Through Seasons

As seasons change, the stories flow,
From winter's chill to summer's glow.
An older tree with creaky limbs,
Shares tales of snowmen who wore whims.

Raccoons debate which nut's a snack,
While owls hoot, leaning back.
Each season spins a brand new tale,
Of pranks in spring or snowy gales.

One branch sways, a cheeky tease,
"Remember that time we caught a breeze?"
The wind just giggles, dances along,
As laughter fills the forest song.

From all around, the whispers blend,
Nature's jesters, a lively trend.
With every rustle and gentle sway,
Stories bound through night and day.

Harmonies Among the Branches

In harmony, the branches sway,
With critters chirping in their play.
A turtle joins, all slow and grand,
Singing songs about the land.

The wind carries a comedic tune,
While bees are buzzing 'neath the moon.
A badger jokes, with quite a grin,
"Who said flying high was a sin?"

A lizard struts, all decked in flair,
As frogs leap in from everywhere.
Together they forge a melody,
In this woodland symphony, so free.

With every rustle, laugh, and cheer,
The stories echo, far and near.
Under the sprawling canopies wide,
Find joy where nature's jokes abide.

Stories Etched in the Earth

Once there stood a tree so bright,
Its roots whispered tales at night.
Squirrels gathered, formed a band,
Sharing gossip, oh so grand!

A raccoon danced, with quite the flair,
While rabbits stopped to laugh and stare.
Tales of acorns, feasts and foes,
The tree grinned wide, as everyone knows.

Its bark would giggle when they cheered,
Almost as if it truly feared.
“Stop your giggling, I’m quite old!
But these stories? They’re pure gold!”

And so the stories spread like fire,
To critters great, and small, and dire.
Each ring within held laughter's sound,
In that tall tree, joy was found!

The Heartbeat of the Olden Tree

In a grove where laughter flowed,
An old tree sat, with tales bestowed.
Its heart would thump with rhythm sweet,
As critters joined for comic feats.

A turtle slipped, oh what a sight!
Fell in a pond, to the frogs' delight.
"Do it again!" cried a wise old crow,
"Do you know how funny you've become, though?"

The whispers of leaves laughed with glee,
At squirrel standing on one small knee.
"Shall we dance?" yelled a chipmunk, spry,
The tree chimed in, "Don't be shy!"

With clever jests and laughter pealed,
The woodland's secrets had revealed.
Beneath the branches, life was bright,
Each heartbeat echoed pure delight!

Ancestral Voices in the Wind

Old leaves rustled with laughter and cheer,
As shadows of past critters appeared.
"Did you hear about the cat so sly?
Thought it could fly, and then—oh my!"

Grandpa Badger with tales so tall,
Sparks of mischief in every call.
"Why did the bird cross the brook?
To tease the fish, oh take a look!"

Their stories danced on the warm spring breeze,
Tickling branches, causing them to tease.
An acorn dropped, "Watch out below!"
And the tree chuckled with a hearty glow.

So gather around, young and old,
For cherished tales that should be told.
Each gust of wind, a memory shared,
In nature's laughter, everyone cared!

Timeless Tales Underneath the Shade

Under the branches, a party would start,
With critters sharing from the heart.
“Did you hear about the frog that croaked?
He tried to sing, but everyone choked!”

The sun shone down like a spotlight bright,
As shadows danced in pure delight.
A merry band of gophers sang,
And the tree’s laughter rang and rang!

With beetles drumming on hollow wood,
They'd tell of adventures that no one could.
“Remember the time we stole some cheese?
Oh, the look on that mouse—priceless tease!”

So don’t forget to stop and play,
Beneath the shade, let worries sway.
For timeless tales of joy will cling,
In every whisper that the tree can bring!

The Elder’s Quiet Narratives

In the glade where whispers dwell,
Old bark grins with tales to tell.
Squirrels laugh at ancient pranks,
As crickets join in silent thanks.

A raccoon with a knowing smirk,
Shares secrets of the woodland work.
While rabbits roll their eyes in glee,
At every wild, unwritten spree.

The breeze carries chuckles near,
From grassy spaces filled with cheer.
Beneath the shade, all creatures lean,
To hear the jests of gray and green.

With roots deep and respect wide,
The wise old guardian cannot hide.
In every rustle, every sigh,
He breathes laughter as time goes by.

Chronicles of the Silent Watcher

A tree stands tall, with a silent grin,
As the forest creatures gather in.
A flamboyant bird, bright with flair,
Sings of mishaps that fill the air.

Bees buzzing with their busy lives,
Share stories of who swerves and dives.
While turtles argue slowest pace,
The tree just chuckles at the race.

An owl hoots in jest so wise,
Telling of gaffes in disguise.
While mice chime in with squeaky glee,
In a raucous dance around the tree.

As shadows stretch and laughter flows,
The watcher knows how each tale goes.
Through seasons passing, stories save,
In this leafy book, we all behave.

The Wisdom of the Woodland

In a grove where the wise ones play,
Leaves gossip about the day.
Chattering critters in a ring,
Share antics like it's the spring.

With a crow who jests and caws with might,
He tells of mishaps in flight.
While hedgehogs roll in roly-poly cheer,
Each stumble graced with laughter clear.

A wise old fox sits with a wink,
As squirrels stop to pause and think.
He offers a tale of clumsy dance,
That leaves them all in a merry trance.

So gather close, in this leafy hall,
Where wisdom wrapped in laughter calls.
In the woodland's embrace, you'll find delight,
As stories come to life at night.

The Archive of Forgotten Treasures

In the shadows of the sprawling trees,
Rest tales buried by the breeze.
Acorns chuckle, while leaves sway,
Bringing back those wild, lost days.

A chipmunk squeaks, “Guess what I found!
A story lost, now spinning round!”
With a hop and a skip, he leads the way,
To forgotten tales that still play.

Old knots and gnarled roots agree,
The buried treasures come with glee.
With each rustle, a new reveal,
A panorama of laughter—what a deal!

So come, dear friends, let’s share a part,
Of eccentric tales that warm the heart.
For in this archive, laughter reigns,
Where every folly is worth the gains.

Resonance of Roots in History

Once a nut that knew it all,
Dreams of grandeur made it tall.
Squirrels listened day and night,
To tales about its treehouse flight.

When sunlight doused the park with glow,
The older branches shared their woe.
They laughed, swapping lies, quite absurd,
About the time they danced with birds.

A modern twist, those roots did boast,
Of ancient feasts with woodland toast.
Each leaf a page, each branch a tale,
Of crazy winds and ships that sail.

Now every critter stops and thrills,
To hear the myths of leafy hills.
A wacky place where truth unspools,
In every whisper, laughter rules!

The Silent Sentinel's Legacy

In silence stood a trunk so grand,
With stories etched across the land.
It chuckled low at passing deer,
Who thought it wise, or maybe queer.

A whisper here, a giggle there,
It joked with shadows, light as air.
'Though I don’t talk,' said bark so tough,
'I’ve seen some things that are quite rough.'

The owls would wink, the raccoons nod,
Sharing secrets that were quite odd.
As clouds would drift and sunlight beam,
The tree would laugh at every dream.

When autumn called, its colors bright,
All creatures joined in pure delight.
In every branch, a snippet glows,
From ancient roots, the fun still flows!

From Seedling to Saga

From tiny seed beneath the rain,
It dreamed of stories, joys, and pain.
Sprouting tall with twisting might,
It juggled acorns, what a sight!

The grass grew green with cheeky glee,
As ants performed their antics free.
'I'll tell you all,' the tree would say,
'Of laughing bugs who tickled play.'

Old tales of storms that tried to sway,
Of dancing storms that came to play.
Friends all around, a lively crowd,
Echoed stories, swift and loud.

With every breeze, the tales would soar,
Of time well spent and laughter galore.
Branching out with every plot,
The tales it spun, forgot not!

Narratives of the Ancient Boughs

In shade so cool, beneath the sky,
The boughs would wriggle, twirl, and sigh.
They shared with leaves, a fun charade,
Of pranks that squirrelly pals had made.

'Once I met a bee on cue,
Who thought my bark was a fancy shoe!
He buzzed and spun, then took a dive,
A true mishap, but oh, he thrived!'

With groans and laughs, they spun the yarn,
Of daisies that wore little horns.
While whispers swirled around so light,
The teasing breeze would join the flight.

Ever since the roots began,
With every tale, the laughter ran.
For every bough hosted a cheer,
In memories thick, the fun was clear!

Whispers in the Canopy

In the branches high, secrets gathered,
A squirrel exclaimed, "I’m rather flattered!"
The leaves giggled, swirling with delight,
As birds shared tales of their late-night flight.

Beneath the shade, a raccoon pranced,
"Dancing with shadows, I've truly advanced!"
A worm rolled its eyes, with a smirk on its face,
"Don’t get too proud; you're still in my space!"

Chronicles of the Ancient Trunk

The mighty trunk leaned, eager to share,
Stories of squirrels and raccoons with flair.
"Did I tell you about the fox with a hat?"
"Oh, do tell again! Was it yellow or flat?"

A snail chimed in, pondering quite soft,
"Did you hear the one about the turtle who scoffed?"
The stories flowed like sap in spring,
With laughter and giggles in everything.

Tales Beneath the Branches

Beneath the lush green, a party was set,
With acorns for snacks and a toothy pet.
The dogs told tales of chasing their tails,
While cats rolled their eyes at all of the fails.

A chipmunk recounted a race with a bee,
"I could have won if it weren't for my knee!"
With chuckles aplenty, the stories took flight,
As shadows danced wildly in the dimming light.

Echoes of Time in Leaves

Leaves stretched their limbs in a swirling spree,
"Remember that time we couldn’t see?"
An owl hooted back, chuckling above,
"In fog so thick, we were lost, but in love!"

A chatter of crickets joined in the fun,
"Let’s not forget when the rain started to run!"
Dance in the chaos, sway with the breeze,
Time far too silly to take with such ease.

Lullabies of the Living Timber

In a forest glade, where giggles play,
The whispers weave tales in a playful sway.
Squirrels tell secrets in nutty delight,
While the shadows dance under moon's silver light.

Beneath leafy arms, a napping bird sings,
Of mishaps and fun, and other wild things.
A raccoon recites from an acorn-stuffed book,
Of treasures and trinkets, come take a look!

Bouncing bunnies share tales of old,
Of adventures so silly, and legends so bold.
While ants in a line play a shuffle dance,
As the trees sway with laughter, in a natural trance.

The wind interrupts with a tickling breeze,
Bringing stories alive, as it rustles the leaves.
In this timbered haven, life’s a merry jest,
Where roots have a chuckle, and moss feels blessed.

Stories That Shelter the Brave

Beneath sturdy boughs where mischief abounds,
Brave critters gather, sharing giggly sounds.
A hedgehog in armor tells tales of his fight,
With bravado and puns that tickle the night.

The whispers of branches form riddles galore,
As toads croak the legends of frogs that once swore,
To hop over streams, but fell with a splash,
Creating a spectacle, oh what a crash!

A wise old owl rolls its eyes in despair,
At stories so wild, one wouldn't dare.
Yet laughter erupts from each feathered friend,
For the bravest souls find joy without end.

Together they cackle 'neath the starlit dome,
Where epic tales spin in their leafy home.
And as dawn breaks, they promise anew,
More stories await, with a comedic view.

The Legacy of Well-Worn Roots

Down in the dirt where stories conspire,
Old roots whisper jokes that never tire.
They've seen all the antics of critters in jest,
Like the time that the squirrel wore a nut on its crest.

Laughed on by the ferns that sway with delight,
While the chuckling mushrooms glow softly at night.
They share tales of the birds with the big fancy hats,
And their dance-offs with beetles, oh what silly spats!

Stick bugs in tuxedos do a waltz in the glade,
With the playful breeze providing the aid.
While slugs gather 'round to cheer and to root,
For the great legacy grows from each friendly shoot.

In laughter and love, their spirits entwine,
As stories take flight on the whispering vine.
What a colorful world, in this life they create,
Where humorous roots decide every fate.

Emanations from the Elder Grove

In the heart of the grove where the gnarled trees wait,
Tales unfold with a chuckle, just tempting fate.
The owls spin yarns, quirks wrapped in humor,
As they nudge at the moon, causing quite the rumor!

A fox in a bowtie struts with great flair,
Telling tall tales of eskimo bears.
The cats chase their tails, claiming trophy galore,
While crickets join in with a melodious score.

With a cackle like thunder, the whispers persist,
Of adventures so wild, they can't be dismissed.
Each branch is a stage, with performers so bright,
Under laughter's embrace, everything feels right.

So linger awhile, as the stories unfold,
In the elder grove, where the weird meets the bold.
For laughter is nurtured in this splendid retreat,
Where every little tale dances to its own beat.

Echoes of Elders in Green

In the woods stood a tree so spry,
It swayed and giggled as folks walked by.
With bark like a book and leaves like a pen,
It knew all the gossip that traveled the glen.

Squirrels would tap it with a jaunty cheer,
“Tell us a tale, oh wise one, come near!”
And the branches would rustle with playful delight,
As the sun dipped low, turning gold from white.

“Have you heard 'bout the rabbit who danced?”
Or the fox who once thought he could prance?
The stories grew taller with each passing year,
While acorns dropped in giggles we’d hear.

So next time you stroll where the whispers begin,
Look for the tree with a mischievous grin.
It’s more than just wood, it’s a jester in green,
With talking roots and a heart ever keen.

The Timeless Chronicles of Wood and Wind

Once a tree stood, quite regal and wide,
With stories inside that could not be tried.
It chuckled to critters, both large and small,
“Gather 'round, friends! I’ve got tales for you all!”

A bird perched up high, with feathers all bright,
Said, “Tell me the secret of the moonlit night!”
“Ah, that’s an old tale of a cat and a kite,
Who danced in the sky till the dawn’s golden light!”

The raccoons chimed in, with their masks and their flair,
“Spin us a yarn of the bear’s great affair!”
“Oh, such a romance!” the tree laughed with glee,
“It involved honey and dancing by three!”

As the breeze played tricks, turning whispers to sound,
The tree let out chuckles that echoed around.
For beneath all the bark and the sturdy facade,
Lurks a poet in nature, that no one can prod.

Whispers of Ancient Roots

Beneath the boughs where the shadows play,
An old one chuckled, “What’s happening today?”
With roots intertwining like gossiping mates,
It shared stories of mischief, of tricks, and of fates.

“Have you heard 'bout the badger with style?”
“He wore a top hat and danced quite awhile!”
The creatures all gathered, the laughter would swell,
As the winds carried whispers of old woodland spells.

A fox raised a paw and howled with a grin,
“Who’s the best dancer? Let the contest begin!”
And the tree smiled wide, its branches in tune,
As the forest erupted with joy ’neath the moon.

So when you come wandering, keep your ears free,
For stories are swirling as wild as the sea.
With each playful breeze and each rustling leaf,
Lies a world full of laughter, of joy, and belief.

Tales Beneath the Canopy

In a glade full of giggles, a tree took the stage,
With legends so funny, it looked like a sage.
“Gather, oh creatures, come listen and cheer,
For the best thing about stories is bringing you near!”

A turtle pressed close, adjusting his specs,
“Is it time for the saga of the dancing hex?”
The tree shook its branches, “Oh yes! Come let’s see,
How he tangled his legs just to mimic a bee!”

The owls hooted loud, and the rabbits all twitched,
As new tales unraveled, each gag well-stitched.
“Now listen, my friends, there’s a twist to this plot,
The bee was a bear, but don’t tell the cops!”

So if you’re out roaming, just stop for a chat,
With the tree in the glen, where tales go splat!
For the laughter it offers, like leaves, it will swirl,
With stories so silly, they’ll give you a twirl.

Legends Etched in Bark

Once a squirrel made quite a fuss,
Claiming the tree was home to a bus.
He painted it bright with berries and goo,
Believing it drove off to buy him a shoe.

A wise old owl, quite full of glee,
Told the tales of a bee who danced like a sea.
In circles and swirls, honey everywhere,
Making the birds giggle; oh what a rare affair!

A rabbit once came, with a tale so bold,
Said he'd won carrots worth their weight in gold.
But the truth was he borrowed them from a friend,
Now those carrots fast vanished, much to his end.

As the seasons change and leaves turn brown,
Each critter spins myths that flip the crown.
Legends unfold in a whirl of delight,
In the funny old tree that sees day and night.

Myths Carved in Silhouette

A raccoon once claimed he was a knight,
Fighting off shadows from morning to night.
With a trash can lid as armor so grand,
He chased off the cats, or so he had planned.

A chipmunk who thought he could truly fly,
Wore a leaf cape and leapt high to the sky.
He landed in mud but didn't lose his cheer,
"Just testing the waters," he said with a sneer!

A skunk with a story that tickled the nose,
Swore he could talk to the squirrels and crows.
"Come join my campfire, we'll share tales galore,"
But all ran away, shouting, "Not anymore!"

In shadows and laughter, legends collide,
With creatures and stories, they take it in stride.
Each carved silhouette a whimsical play,
In an ancient tree's heart, where spirits will stay.

The Eldest Guardian's Chronicles

An acorn once dreamed of reigning as king,
With branches for arms, he'd dance and he'd sing.
He'd rule over ferns, the mushrooms, and grass,
But grew into something a little more crass.

A nimble-footed fox with a view of the land,
Declared he'd outsmart everyone, just as he planned.
But tripping on roots, his scheme was uncorked,
And laughter erupted as he proudly snorted.

An elderly tortoise sat high up in boughs,
Telling tall tales while the creatures all wowed.
"I once ran a race against lightning and wind,
But forgot where I started, it's where I descend!"

Chronicles flutter in the soft summer air,
With each giggle echoing stories to share.
The eldest guardian chuckles, quite proud,
As myths spin around him, both silly and loud.

Stories Twined with Vines

Little lizards in costumes parade up and down,
They built a grand float made of leaves, quite a crown.
With twigs for their fans, it was quite a display,
Though singing off-key made the frogs leap away.

A raccoon in glasses proclaimed he could teach,
How to fish without putting a paw in the reach.
But with nets made of grass, he snared only air,
And each failed attempt made them all stop and stare.

The fireflies sparkled, they formed a conga line,
As the moon cheered them on with a wink and a shine.
They danced through the night, under stars so divine,
Spinning stories and laughter twined with the vines.

Each creature alive with a heart full of glee,
Crafting their tales in glorious spree.
In the shadowy coils where memories grow,
Fun stories are woven, come witness the show!

Sentinels of the Stories Untold

In the woods where whispers play,
Trees gossip in their sway.
One claims to know a bear,
Forever stuck in a fuzzy chair.

Squirrels gather with a grin,
Hearing tales of where they've been.
Acorns drop like applause,
For the mysteries in their paws.

A raccoon rolls his eyes,
Laughing at the birdies' cries.
'What's a nest without a mess?'
The trees chuckle, they're the best!

With branches waving side to side,
They share tales with twisted pride.
Every creak is a chuckle,
In this leafy little huddle.

Roots of the Past

Deep below where shadows dwell,
Roots conspire, oh so well.
One swears he saw a shoe,
From a traveler who overgrew.

Digging up a picnic spread,
Grubs sing songs of crumbs they fed.
Every scoop, a laugh indeed,
As they chatter ‘bout the need.

Forgotten stories, buried bright,
Glimpse of silliness in the night.
A legend of a juggler's fall,
Told by roots, embraced by all.

They wiggle and twist with delight,
Poking fun at tree-swinging flight.
For every slip, a hearty cheer,
In the earth, they laugh sincere.

Branches of Tomorrow

Stretching out with hopeful dreams,
The branches play in sunlight beams.
One dreams to be a swing,
While another thinks of everything.

Leaves giggle in the breeze,
Sharing tales that bring heart's ease.
A plan for hats or perhaps a boat,
With fluttering thoughts, they all gloat.

The saplings dance in sunlit glee,
Imagining what they will be.
A treehouse, castle, or a clown,
With laughter echoing all around.

Whimsical visions swirl and twirl,
Each branch a twist, a joyful whirl.
In the sky, their dreams take flight,
Branches giggling, pure delight.

Windswept Whispers of Wisdom

The gusty breeze brings giggles near,
Swaying branches, spreading cheer.
A wise old twig shouts, 'Listen close!',
'It's not a tree; it's a furry host!'

Leaves flutter like little flags,
With secrets stored in their bags.
'This one's for the squirrel on a diet,
Who thinks nuts are his soy-fried riot!'

Twisting tales blow through the air,
An acorn's tale of love and flair.
'Plant me somewhere, take a chance,'
And across the wind, the branches dance.

Echoes of laughter swirl and weave,
Windsplay whispers may mislead.
Yet every rustle brings a twist,
To make you giggle, none can resist!

Chronicles of the Canopied Keep

In a kingdom of leaves and bark,
Legends roam from dawn till dark.
Squirrels overlap in a regal chat,
Debating over acorn's latest spat.

Every crown boasts a wacky claim,
Of a bird who fancied the name.
'The Ruler of the Snatch and Grab!'
The canopy bursts out in a jab.

Breezes carry their tales anew,
Of mischief and things they'll pursue.
'Last week, I took a nap mid-hike,'
Said a branch that loves to spike!

Bathed in sun, they laugh and cheer,
Holding court with a joyful leer.
Chronicles ride the mighty wind,
In this realm, silliness won't rescind!

www.ingramcontent.com/pod-product-compliance
Lightning Source LLC
Chambersburg PA
CBHW072143200426
43209CB00051B/330
9781805672883